RAVING BEAUTIES

# IN THE PINK

*Illustrated by*
*Anne Christie and Liz Dalton*

 The Women's Press

First published by The Women's Press Limited 1983
A member of the Namara Group
124 Shoreditch High Street, London E1 6JE

Introduction and collection copyright © Raving Beauties Limited

British Library Cataloguing in Publication Data

In the pink.
    1.  Women authors—English poetry—Women authors
    I.  Raving Beauties
    821′.008′09287        PR1177

    ISBN 0-7043-3920-X

Typeset by MC Typeset, Chatham, Kent
Printed in Great Britain by Nene Litho
and bound by Woolnough Bookbinding,
both of Wellingborough, Northants

The Raving Beauties gratefully acknowledge permission from the
following to reprint the poems in this book:

Peter Owen Ltd, Michael Impey and Brian Swann for 'The Ordeal' by
Nina Cassian and 'The Assignation' by Juana de Ibarbourou, both
published in *An Anthology of Contemporary Rumanian Poetry*; Ruth
Feldman and Brian Swann for their translation of 'Birth' by Edith
Bruck; Swallow Press, Chicago, for 'Notes from the Delivery Room'
by Linda Pastan; Olwen Hughes Literary Agency for 'Morning Song',
'Child' and 'The Applicant' by Sylvia Plath, all from *Ariel*, copyright
Ted Hughes 1963, published by Faber & Faber, London; Alta for 'this
day has been the craps', 'your tiny body warms my breast', 'you fell
asleep drinking', 'you touch yr navel – whazzat?', 'I wake feeling your
hand', 'a long time/distance from home', 'I would write a love story',
'penus envy, they call it', 'why do you write they ask', 'I stepped into
the ring', 'what of the lonely 7-year-old', 'o i do want to do it all i

*From* The Women's Press Ltd
124 Shoreditch High Street, London E1

*RAVING BEAUTIES (from top):*

*Anna Carteret* has spent most of her life working in the theatre, particularly at the National Theatre, where she played many leading parts between 1967 and 1982. Her television credits include two recent plays, *Being Normal* and *Change Partners*, in which she plays two different mothers. Perhaps she is best known as the Police Inspector in the BBC television series *Juliet Bravo*.

*Fanny Viner* has worked as an actress and a teacher. Her acting career includes seasons with the Royal Shakespeare Company and the National Theatre.

*Sue Jones-Davies*, a former member of the Bowles Brothers Band, has acted in theatrical productions ranging from *Jesus Christ Superstar* to *Othello*. Her television credits include *Rock Follies, Lloyd George* and *How Green Was My Valley* (the last two set in her native Wales). She has also appeared in the films *The Life of Brian, Radio On* and *Newid Gêr*.

*IN THE PINK:*

Old Red Lion, June 1981; Riverside Studios, August 1981; National Theatre, December 1981; Battersea Arts Centre, February 1982; Bath Festival, May 1982; Edinburgh Festival, August 1982; Albany Empire, October 1982; International Festival of Sitges (Lysistrata Prize), October 1982; Broadcast on Channel 4's opening night, October 1982.

'Witty, angry, literary, funny, clever, entertaining, provocative' Ray Conolly in the *Standard*

'Essential and startling viewing' *City Limits*

'(brilliant, actually)' Bel Mooney in the *Observer*

want', and '& all those years' (from 'Placenta Praevia'), copyright ©
Alta, c/o Shameless Hussy Press, Berkeley, California, 1971, 1983;
Anne Stevenson for 'The Suburb', published in *Travelling Behind
Glass*, Oxford University Press, Oxford, 1974; and 'Poem to My
Daughter' from *Minute by Glass Minute*, Oxford University Press,
1982; Lucille Clifton, c/o Curtis Brown Ltd, New York, for 'The Lost
Baby Poem'; Michelene Wandor for 'I'll be Mother', copyright
Michelene Wandor, first published in *Upbeat*, by Journeyman Press,
London; The Sterling Lord Agency, New York, for 'Pain for a
Daughter' by Anne Sexton, published in *Live or Die* by Anne Sexton,
1966, Houghton Mifflin, New York; and for 'The Long Tunnel of
Wanting You', 'Aging', 'Back to Africa', 'The Truce Between the
Sexes' and 'Woman Enough' by Erica Jong copyright 1968, 70, 71, 72,
73, 79; Elaine Feinstein for 'At 7 a Son' from *Some Unease & Angels*,
Hutchinson & Co., London 1977; Fran Landesman for 'Do a Dance
for Daddy' from *Invade My Privacy,* Jonathan Cape, London, 1978;
James MacGibbon for 'Mother' by Stevie Smith, from *The Collected
Poems of Stevie Smith*, Allen Lane, London; Maya Angelou for 'Men';
Anthony Sheil Associates for 'The Woman in the Ordinary', 'Rape
Poem' and 'In the Men's Room(s)' by Marge Piercy, copyright © 1982
by Marge Piercy, from *Circles in the Water*, published by Alfred A
Knopf, New York; New Directions, New York, for 'To the Tune of
"Red Embroidered Shoes" ' by Huang O, from Kenneth Rexroth,
*Women Poets of China*. Copyright © 1972 by Kenneth Rexroth and Ling
Chung. Reprinted by permission of New Directions Publishing
Corporation; Stephanie Smolensky for 'I Told You When We Started
This Relationship', first published in *Spare Rib*, London; Nikki
Giovanni for 'Seduction', copyright © 1968, from *Black Feeling, Black
Talk/Black Judgment*, by permission of the author; Joan Larkin, for
'Vagina Sonnet', copyright © 1975, first published in *Housework*, Out
& Out Books, New York; Gerald Duckworth & Co Ltd for 'Penelope'
by Dorothy Parker, from *The Collected Dorothy Parker*; Joanna
Bankier and Rabén & Sjögren, Stockholm, for 'The Marital Problem'
by Sonja Akesson; New Directions for 'The Ache of Marriage' by
Denise Levertov, from *O Taste and See*; Alison Fell for 'In Confidence'
and 'Period Madness', both from *Smile, Smile, Smile, Smile*, Sheba
Feminist Publishers, London, 1980; Barbara A Zanditon and Only-
women Press, London, for 'This Year . . .', from *One Foot on the
Mountain*, Onlywomen Press, 1979; Astra, for 'Bloody Pause' and
'Back You Come'; Maureen Burge for 'The Diet', first published in
*Bread and Roses*, Virago, London; Lisel Mueller for 'A Nude by

Edward Hopper', published in *Rising Tides*, Washington Square Press, c/o Simon & Schuster, New York; Susan Griffin for 'Three Poems for Women', 'An Answer to a Man's Question', 'A Woman Defending Herself', 'The Woman Who Swims in Her Tears', 'The Frozen Sea', 'White Bear' and 'Love Should Grow Up Like a Wild Iris in the Fields', copyright © Susan Griffin 1967–76; Robin Morgan for the excerpt from '*Monster: Poems by Robin Morgan*', copyright © Robin Morgan 1972, published by Random House/Vintage Books, New York, 1972: excerpted with permission from the author; Aspen and Onlywomen Press for 'For my "Apolitical" Sisters', from *One Foot On the Mountain*, Onlywomen Press, London 1979; George Braziller Inc for 'Objets d'Art' by Cynthia MacDonald, from *No More Masks*, Braziller, New York; Susan Saxe for 'Questionnaire' from 'Trilogy . . . Notes from the First Year', published in *Talk Among the Women-folk*, copyright © Susan Saxe; Kath McKay and Onlywomen Press for 'To Phil If He Wakes Up'; Beacon Press, Boston, and Judith Hemschemeyer for 'The Petals of the Tulip', from *Tangled Vines*, Beacon Press, Boston; Mary Dorcey for 'First Love' from *Bread and Roses,* Virago, London; Judith McDaniel for 'For My Mother's Mother', from *So's Your Old Lady*, December 1975; Random house for 'Miss Rosie' by Lucille Clifton; from *Good Times*; Michèle Roberts for 'Magnificat' from *Bread and Roses*, Virago, London; Sharon Barba for 'Thanksgiving', from *Rising Tides*, Washington Square Press; Grace Schulman and *The Nation* Associates for 'To Julia de Burgos', published in *A Book of Woman Poets from Antiquity to Now*, Beacon Press, Boston; Jaakko A Ahokas for his translation of 'A Decision' by Edith Södergran.

*The Illustrations*

The drawings of the Raving Beauties in performance are by Liz Dalton; the drawings of the Raving Beauties at home are by Anne Christie.

Illustrations on pages 23, 40, 46, 56–57, 60, 66 and 85 copyright © Liz Dalton 1983

Illustrations on pages 15, 31, 33, 77, 92, 98, 112, 118, 126–7 copyright © Anne Christie 1983

# Contents

*In The Pink* would not have been possible without the friend-ship and support of the following people:

Milli Kosoy Gervasi
Dee Welding
Sally Flemington

Lol Schenck
Denise Ruben
Saffy Ashtiany

and

Barbara Rosenblat
Jacky Stoller
Barbara Derkow
Lucie and Annie La Paz
Charlie Hanson
Michael Mayhew
Margaret Fisher
Kerry Bignell
Pete Atkins

Colin Sell
Charmine Dawkins
Sarah Finch
Greg Hicks
Chris Langham
Christopher Morahan
Bill Colleran
Marta Pessarrodona
Stella Maris

The National Theatre
Riverside Studios

The British Council
Channel Four

# Foreword

Fan:

The Raving Beauties are Anna Carteret, Sue Jones-Davies and myself, Fanny Viner.

I am a grateful feminist, although that adjective is not easily associated with feminism. The movement wasn't born out of finding things to be grateful for. But I am grateful because, having attracted chaos and hell through my relationships with men, I am waving, not drowning. This book is about that power in women, expressed in our poetry. Other women in history have broken through the dam that holds us, but our anthology bears witness to the fact that the modern women's movement has made the trickle of rebellion a flood.

In The Pink was the theatrical programme of songs and poetry by and about women that we put together. It started life in a pub, was a sell-out at the Edinburgh Festival in 1982, won the Lysistrata Prize at Sitges, and was broadcast on the first night of Channel 4. It was the piece of work in all our diverse careers for which we felt entirely responsible, and which we most love. Its success enabled us to acknowledge an achievement that was our own.

We were not the originators of our material: we owe everything to the women who wrote the poetry we perform. But the selection was totally personal, our commitment to the material making the long hours of research and discussion a joy. And the poetry in turn was given life and energy by us, by our performance.

In The Pink's reception, and the spate of letters we received after it was broadcast, showed that we had tapped a source of feeling common to thousands of women. This anthology is an opportunity to share our experience of these poems even more widely, and to add others.

The seed of In The Pink was sown after I had spent one and a half years at home, looking after my daughter Alex. I did not know how much I was repressing at the time, but now I love Alta and Susan Griffin for their courage in sharing their feelings of violence, pain and anger about those early years of child-rearing, and so putting me in touch with my own:

> & all those years nobody loved me
> except her & I screamed at her & spanked
> her
> & threw her on the bed & slammed the
> door when
> I was angry & desperate for her
> father's love.

It was in this mood of frustration that I wrote to Sue, who is for me the perfect blend of seriousness and fun, and suggested that we put together a cabaret act of songs. I had no idea how healing the work would be.

We decided to arrange our songs as 'Everywoman's Love Story', and that was as far as we'd got when we were introduced to Anna. Her English-rose appearance belied her practical intuitive intelligence and a will of iron. Anna also wanted to do a show, based on women's poetry. So the poetry joined the songs, and we became a threesome.

The six months that it took to put In The Pink together were chaotic, always surrounded by domestic mess and sometimes the claims of other professional work. For Anna and me, 'tea-time' became a pretext to get together and discuss poetry. Our books shared space with abandoned crusts of marmite and toast ('I don't want curly hair!'), while the children played and grizzled together. It was a wonderful demonstration of how women keep it all going at once: the fine thread of intellectual concentration and the ceaseless, unpredictable demands of

12

children. During much of this time Sue was working in Wales, and also finding time to send us poems for consideration.

At school, I had been *taught* my responses to poetry, so that it was made dry and academic, and me insensitive and stupid. However, certain pieces could not be killed off entirely, and the poetry I loved then I shall always love: Keats, Wordsworth, Milton, Browning. I hardly encountered any women poets, even at university, taught by the glorious Germaine Greer.

Poetry has become divorced from our lives. We no longer feel part of the great oral and written tradition of myths and legends in which so many things were once protected and preserved. Nothing protects us, our minds, bodies and spirits are freely raped in the age of atomic suicide. The eternal truths of language have given way to momentary flickerings on a video tape.

Although Keats' nightingale has not stopped singing for me, women's poetry has introduced me to more immediate, mundane metaphors for the bitter-sweet life, in which sex can condemn as cruelly as time.

In discussing the truth of the poetry we were of course discussing our own truth. There were barriers to be broken through, barriers to do with the feelings our culture denies. Some were about our suppressed female rage against men; some about our denied love of women.

Performing the 'rage' poems surprised me with the intensity of the anger I was enabled to express: I BLAME you for my misery – it is *your* world and it is loveless and violent – I shall destroy the destroyer! My hatred empowers me, I am become a goddess, a fury, I squat on the earth, fluids pour from my cunt, seas and blood . . . To get in touch with one's hatred, anger and violence can be a heady release, and several poems in the anthology draw on the power that allowing anger can give. Even when the anger is in part diffused by humour, there is no denying Kath McKay's intention:

>Anger
>Anger drove me to it
>I killed him at last.

13

I loved performing that poem. She remains so innocent. If only hatred could always be disposed of so casually!

How the new-found power and expressiveness of women will affect men, I don't know. I know that women have been the secret army servicing the world, and I have loathed being one of its ranks. One of my greatest achievements in recent years has been to tolerate unmoved, passionless, the sight of cobwebs hanging from my ceiling. The Bacchantes had to throw down their hoovers before they could join Dionysus in his carnally innocent revels. We cannot *exchange* womanhood for personhood. Breast and cunt endure. We must go into the beauty of womanhood, not get out of it. As for men, our escape from prison will make the warder redundant.

Women's poetry on the other hand took us into our feelings for women. None of us is lesbian, but we discovered a profound response to lesbian poetry. I have experienced that fearless compassion that can exist between women, and have a special reverence for Susan Griffin's women who cry out in joy together.

Because of the compression of thought and feeling in poetry, it takes time to read and experience. It is enough to linger over a few lines, and the truth in them can suddenly put together the unconscious sensations of a lifetime. One of the poems in which this happened for me was Judith McDaniel's 'For My Mother's Mother'. It speaks of the isolation of women in their 'female' experiences, an isolation which has been our unspoken common bond. And for most of us, that isolation has been experienced in relation to men.

No wonder so many of our poets write of birth. Until I had my children, I had not considered how I would fulfil the role of 'woman' in a nuclear family. The poets we performed have helped me to accept that though I love my children I will not sacrifice myself for them, and I don't think that is what they need. There is a death and rebirth in every birth. Through giving birth a woman touches the razor edge of life itself, she understands its unstoppable energy, its heart-searing fragility. Yet for so many of us, those most extravagant gifts of birth and

bleeding end up as life-diminishers. They do not empower, they enslave.

Further, I am no longer merely *grateful* to be working. It is my right, as well as a practical necessity. I will never put my life in the hands of a man – it is far too precious. As Jill Johnson said at Town Bloody Hall, 'You can have my body when I've finished with it'.

Yet I still find the lack of male support daunting, demoralising. Is Father not as important a role as Mother? Allocating blame no longer seems useful. Our ability to have visions, to fantasise a better life, may be the only dignity we have left.

In the anthology we have included poetry about male vulnerability, love-filled fucks, male tears and dreams and humour. Forced out of romantic fantasy, coming through loneliness to a kind of aloneness, there will, as Erica Jong puts it, be trouble enough, but of a different sort.

Vita Sackville West wrote of her husband:

> He has complete power over my heart, though not over my spirit. It is a real tenderness I feel for him, it is a constant sense of 'Tread gently, for you tread upon my dreams.'

Give me her reactionary privileges, and I would have all the time in the world for his heart and *my spirit*!


Anna:

I have always been someone who tried to squeeze the impossible into each day, determined to be at once good mother, wife, friend, teacher, actress; so reading became a luxury. I read poetry because it was brief, but satisfying. And gradually it became part of my everyday life, particularly poetry written by women. I was excited because so many women thought and felt as I did. I longed to share my discoveries: But how? My only talent was as a performer.

On Boxing Day 1980, I met Fanny Viner. I was struck by her unusually direct manner and vivid personality. I mentioned that I was interested in performing poetry, by women, learnt that she and Sue were planning a programme of songs, and somewhere in that conversation emerged the idea of combining the two . . .

Later I met Sue, and liked her immediately. She seemed quiet but positive in a practical, earthy way. And as we began to work together, searching for a theme to contain the material we had found, it became apparent that we stimulated each other's minds and imaginations. But it was not until we were offered a venue, a place and date to perform, that we had actually to commit ourselves. We agreed that it was now, or never.

The first task was to make a final selection, and in this period we became very close. As we grew more confident, there would be arguments about what we as a group were trying to say, and what was most important to us individually. We agreed on excellence as a final criterion: each poem was to be included for its quality, not just because we identified with its content. We forced each other to examine our motives, and our relationship with every poem, and the confrontations we experienced then sharpened our interpretations of the poems in performance.

We learned a great deal from each other in rehearsal. I worked compulsively and had difficulty in letting myself go. Fanny's sheer audacity sometimes inhibited me, and my insistence on rigorous rehearsal in turn irritated her. I admired, and envied, her ability to let her emotions rip, seemingly careless of the damage she might do, then walk on stage and give an amazing performance. I was thankful that my technique enabled me to hide my resentment from the audience – then was reminded by the poetry itself how common to women is this art of hiding our feelings, to such an extent that we have difficulty in releasing our emotions when the need arises. This was one of the threads running through In The Pink.

So we learned *through* the poetry. Interpreting the verse compelled us to open up. We found we simply could not do justice to certain poems without exposing areas of ourselves we usually kept hidden. The honesty of the writing demanded the same commitment from us.

We found a theme beginning with the womb, and tracing a journey through birth, childhood, sexual initiation and relationship, motherhood, separation, maturity, independence. When deciding who should perform which poem, we arrived at the idea of using our three distinct personalities to create three women who would reflect different attitudes to our chosen themes.

Although I had been involved before in political issues concerned with other people's oppression, I had never thought of myself as part of the women's movement until we did In The Pink. So I understood the reproach of Aspen's poem 'For My Apolitical Sisters', in which she describes the unconscious apathy of the woman she addresses:

> when you nurture his ego, offer your body,
> wash his socks, raise his children,
> you are being a political activist too.

Indeed, many of us yearn for the freedom to express and be ourselves, but avoid facing up to it. Robin Morgan urges us to *do* something about it:

> to admit suffering is to begin
> the creation of freedom.

It took me a long time to find the right way of performing this extract from Robin Morgan's 'Monster'. First I tried it angrily, which felt good, but I suspected that I was only succeeding in alienated the audience I wanted to draw into the poem. In the end I put it clearly and unemotionally – reflecting the objectivity inherent in the verse. In a sense, this poem and our understanding of it served as metaphor for our own progress as oppressed women facing up to our situation and learning to deal with our oppression.

Compiling the anthology has enabled us to expand into areas not explored in the show. I was determined to include at least one poem about marriage that would reflect faith in the idea that a husband and lover can be a friend, because that is what I feel I have been fortunate to find in my own marriage. It is striking that we had included nothing positive about marriage in the show. So, I turned to Erica Jong's 'The Truce Between the Sexes'.

We also chose poems around the idea of women's work, our drive to create, our need to work in the world, and the conflicts that arise if we have children. We turned to Alta and Susan Griffin to express that feeling of being torn in half, the guilt that eats away at our consciousness. My two daughters are flourishing, but I still can't get rid of the feeling that my mother may be right and I am not being a 'real mother' to them! It took working on In The Pink to make me realise how much I care about woman's dual needs, to excel at work and at mother-hood. And to see the contradictions in my solution: I work away from home, and employ another woman to be at home while I work. And what of the aspirations of this other woman? It's society as a whole we'll have to change to resolve these contradictions.

Discovering the poets in this book has helped me to be more aware of the conflicts in my own life; working on the poems has enabled me to give expression to my feelings; and com-piling the anthology has broadened and confirmed my empathy with other women. I hope that many more women will share the discoveries we have made.


Sue:

When Fan suggested that we might do some work together, my immediate reaction was one of pure delight. I was out of work at the time, and desperately in need of creative valid-ation. I was busy bringing up a small son (and I know all the arguments for the creative potential in doing that), but there was a whole area of my personality that was not being nurtured. I needed a professional stimulus. The theatre can do terrible things to your ego. You are constantly waiting to be asked, waiting to be wanted, and when the waiting runs into months rather than weeks, you begin to wonder not just 'Am I good enough for the job?' but 'Is there still a me to give a job to?' This identity problem, which affects most actors some of the time, seems to affect most women most of the time! If women are the invisible 50 percent of the world's population, between motherhood and acting I was feeling about as invisible as you can get. Fan's offer was like a life-line.

Fan and I had met at the Chichester Festival. I don't remember much of what we did on stage, but I do have clear and vivid memories of us striding over the South Downs, in very un-fashionable shorts, talking incessantly about personal relation-ships. Fan is an original – which is what makes her so exciting, on stage and off.

Our first venture was very modest. We did two songs for a charity concert. But in terms of a personal breakthrough those two songs were an opera! Work took on a different perspec-tive. It was no longer something 'given' to you. It was some-thing you gave to other people – 'my work'! This transition in my mental outlook from passive to active was a major milestone, although at the time I was not conscious of it. I was just happy that we'd performed our repertoire satisfactorily. I was quite surprised when Anna suggested that we join forces and expand the act by adding poetry to our songs.

I was resistant at first: to the idea of poetry and to Anna too. She seemed so competent and assured, and I couldn't imagine how anyone so organised would fit into our haphazard way of working. However, Anna was and is wonderfully determined, and quite impervious to obstacles. One minute I was unsure about the whole thing; the next I had a sheaf of poems to look through. Anna's thoroughness can still be overpowering, but it was she who galvanised us into doing the show. And now, two years on, instead of being intimidated I revel in her energy and enthusiasm.

My hesitation about the poetry was based on fear. Poetry seemed to demand an honesty in performance which unnerved me. To get to the core of a poem you have to peel away layers, rather like peeling an onion, and in the process you leave yourself exposed.

But once we began to rehearse, my initial fear was replaced by a wonderful sense of release. Because I trusted the others it was possible to strip off emotionally in front of them, and to use the energy usually reserved for putting up defences into doing the work itself.

It was never easy. We all had other commitments: Fan was pregnant with her second baby, Anna had to grab rehearsal time between her other acting work, there were personality clashes. But at my most depressed, the quality of the poems stood out like a beacon and gave me the impetus to go on.

Like Fan and Anna, I found that performing clarified my ideas and feelings. The poems helped to chart my own hesitant growth, and point a way forward. For example, 'Men' and 'Nervous Prostration' both portray women in our all too common role of victim: the young girl in 'Men' is not an active participant in the sex act, it is something done to her, and her only rebellion is independent of her will – 'Your body has slammed shut'. She will probably grow up to be what the world calls 'frigid'. Women frequently hit back at their predicament in ways that only make it worse for themselves. Similarly, the woman in 'Nervous Prostration', starved of love and warmth from the world around her, denies herself emotion and becomes a cut-glass vase, apeing the smothering formality of her environment to the point where she is 'still enough to be dead'. We do a good line in martyrs.

But, although we see women struggling with the old roles, we also see them breaking free to explore new ones, new territories, new patterns of living. That is what is so exciting about the anthology. It has a dynamic, it shows us that we do not stand still. In her poem 'Woman Enough' Erica Jong writes of a reversal of traditional roles:

> I sit at my typewriter
> Remembering my grandmother
> . . . .
> & the man I love cleans up the kitchen.

While Alta's anguished cry 'O I want to do it all' finds an echo in the longing of all of us to defy our limitations. We know it will not be easy. As long as we are women, mothers, daughters, wives, lovers, there will always be struggle and conflict. But out of that will come growth. It helps to know that our personal battles are not conducted alone, that there is a shared vision.

The poem that epitomises what I would like to think of as the essence of this anthology is 'Ordeal'. Its energy is totally life-enhancing. This woman has never heard the words 'victim' and 'passive'. Her sheer vitality opens our eyes to the infinite possibilities of life: only dare!

Poetry really is capable of transforming our vision. For me, the woman in 'Ordeal' was a revelation. If she can do it – with love and support, so can we all.

In the Pink

PROLOGUE

## Ordeal

I promise to make you more alive than you've ever been.
For the first time you'll see your pores opening
like the gills of a fish and you'll hear
the noise of blood in galleries
and feel light gliding on your corneas
like the dragging of a dress across the floor.
For the first time, you'll note gravity's prick
like a thorn in your heel,
and your shoulder blades will hurt from the imperative of
        wings.
I promise to make you so alive that
the fall of dust on furniture will deafen you,
and you'll feel your eyebrows like two wounds forming
and your memories will seem to begin
with the creation of the world.

*Nina Cassian*
*translated by Michael Impey and Brian Swann*

# Birth

Feeling the urge my mother
made for the privy at the far end of the courtyard
and strained strained with all her might
plagued by her painful constipation.
'It's like giving birth,' she kept saying to herself
and strained strained harder
broad forehead dripping sweat
bluegreen eyes full of tears
veins swollen on the white neck
untouched by real or imitation jewels.
The kerchief slipped off
showing her dark hair;
with both hands she held onto the swollen belly with me
        inside.
To readjust her head-covering
like a good Orthodox Jew she let go of her belly
and kept straining straining.
The next thing was a cry a long-drawn-out wail:
my head almost grazed the pit full of excrement.
A busy neighbour woman
ran to her aid and that's how I was born.
According to the gypsies a lucky future was in store for me;
for my father I was another mouth to feed
for my mother an unavoidable calamity
that befalls poor religious couples who make love
as a gesture of peace after months of quarrels
for my five not seven brothers
(luckily two died young)
a real toy that squealed
sucked at the wrinkled nipples
clung to the skin of mama's empty breasts
a mother undernourished like the mothers
of Asia Africa India South
or North America of yesterday today and tomorrow . . .

*Edith Bruck; translated by Ruth Feldman and Brian Swann*

# Notes from the Delivery Room

Strapped down,
victim in an old comic book,
I have been here before,
this place where pain winces
off the walls
like too bright light.
Bear down a doctor says,
foreman to sweating labourer,
but this work, this forcing
of one life from another
is something that I signed for
at a moment when I would have signed anything.
Babies should grow in fields;
common as beets or turnips
they should be picked and held
root end up, soil spilling
from between their toes –
and how much easier it would be later,
returning them to earth.
Bear up . . . bear down . . . the audience
grows restive, and I'm a new magician
who can't produce the rabbit
from my swollen hat.
She's crowning, someone says,
but there is no one royal here,
just me, quite barefoot,
greeting my barefoot child.

*Linda Pastan*

## Morning Song

Love set you going like a fat gold watch.
The midwife slapped your footsoles, and your bald cry
Took its place among the elements.

Our voices echo, magnifying your arrival. New statue
In a draughty museum, your nakedness
Shadows our safety. We stand round blankly as walls.

I'm no more your mother
Than the cloud that distils a mirror to reflect its own slow
Effacement at the wind's hand.

All night your moth-breath
Flickers among the flat pink roses. I wake to listen;
A far sea moves in my ear.

One cry, and I stumble from bed, cow-heavy and floral
In my Victorian nightgown.
Your mouth opens clean as a cat's. The window square

Whitens and swallows its dull stars. And now you try
Your handful of notes;
The clear vowels rise like balloons.

*Sylvia Plath*

# Child

Your clear eye is the one absolutely beautiful thing.
I want to fill it with colour and ducks,
The zoo of the new

Whose names you meditate –
April snowdrop, Indian pipe,
Little

Stalk without wrinkle,
Pool in which images
Should be grand and classical

Not this troublous
Wringing of hands, this dark
Ceiling without a star.

*Sylvia Plath*

this day has been the craps.
i sit on the bed, hunched in despair
& a little fuzzy head rests
on my knee, a tiny hand on my thigh.
your voice a melody. – hi?


your tiny body warms my breast.
my belly relaxes & you rest
your dear head on my shoulder,
little fingers pat my back.


you fell asleep drinking
from my breast, drinking
nourishment & warmth & a
new mothers growing love.
it was not stained glass
windows: it was the pressure
& release of milk from
my body to yours: our
deep communion.


you touch yr navel – whazzat? –
& i pull up my shirt. you stare
delited, poke yr finger
in my belly button, then yours.
– whazzat? whazzat? –

i wake feeling your hand
patting mine, you on tip toes
to see me in bed – hi mommy –
& you have taught me:
love can grow.
day. by day.


a long time/distance from home
holding yr warm dark baby,
she falls asleep in my arms
& i shed silent tears of joy
in the dark bus.

*Alta*

# The Suburb

No time, no time,
and with so many in line to be
born or fed or made love to, there is no
excuse for staring at it, though it's spring again
and the leaves have come out looking
limp and wet like little green new born babies.

The girls have come out in their new bought dresses,
carefully, carefully. They know they're in danger.
Already there are couples crumpled under the chestnuts.
The houses crowd closer, listening to each other's radios.
Weeds have got into the window boxes. The washing
        hangs,
helpless. Children are lusting for ice cream.

It is my lot each May to be hot and pregnant,
a long way away from the years when I slept by myself –
the white bed by the dressing table, pious with cherry
        blossoms,
the flatteries and punishments of photographs and mirrors.
We walked home by starlight and he touched my breasts.
'Please, please!' Then I let him anyway. Cars
droned and flashed, sucking at the cow parsley. Later
there were teas and the engagement party. The wedding
in the rain. The hotel where I slept in the bathroom.
The night when he slept on the floor.

The ache of remembering, bitter as a birth. Better
to lie still and let the babies run through me.
To let them possess me. They will spare me
spring after spring. Their hungers deliver me.
I grow fat as they devour me. I give them my sleep
and they absolve me from waking. Who can accuse me?
I am beyond blame.

*Anne Stevenson*

32

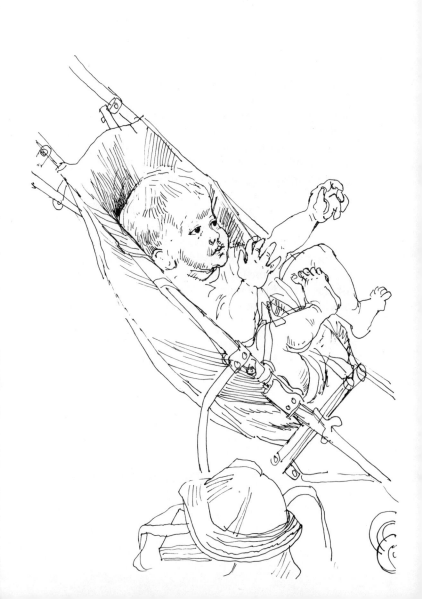

# The Lost Baby Poem

the time i dropped your almost body down
down to meet the waters under the city
and run one with the sewage to the sea
what did i know about waters rushing back
what did i know about drowning
or being drowned

you would have been born into winter
in the year of the disconnected gas
and no car     we would have made the thin
walk over Genesee hill into the Canada wind
to watch you slip like ice into strangers' hands
you would have fallen naked as snow into winter
if you were here i could tell you these
and some other things

if i am ever less than a mountain
for your definite brothers and sisters
let the rivers pour over my head
let the sea take me for a spiller
of seas     let black men call me stranger
always     for your never named sake

*Lucille Clifton*

34

# I'll be Mother

got a cold? she tells me
your nose is running, she suggests
you're tired
you're going to sleep, she says

she would not like me to be dead
because then she would have to grieve

    she just wants me to be asleep
    no trouble,
    just breathing
    so she feels she's done her duty

    that way she won't remember
    the blackout curtains
    the ladder
    the tacks
    the jumping up and down
    from the floor to the chair
    from the chair to the table
    from the table up the ladder
    and the same in reverse
    to make the stubborn foetus
    dislodge in a cloud of unnecessary blood

abortions were rare and dangerous things in those days,
she says

I have a little cold
I shall have a little snooze
and then I'll wake up
so bloody there.

*Michelene Wandor*

# Pain for a Daughter

Blind with love, my daughter
has cried nightly for horses,
those long-necked marchers and churners
that she has mastered, any and all,
reigning them in like a circus hand –
the excitable muscles and the ripe neck;
tending this summer, a pony and a foal.
She who is too squeamish to pull
a thorn from the dog's paw,
watched her pony blossom with distemper,
the underside of the jaw swelling
like an enormous grape.
Gritting her teeth with love,
she drained the boil and scoured it
with hydrogen peroxide until pus
ran like milk on the barn floor.

Blind with loss all winter,
in dungarees, a ski jacket and a hard hat,
she visits the neighbours' stable,
our acreage not zoned for barns;
they who own the flaming horses
and the swan-whipped thoroughbred
that she tugs at and cajoles,
thinking it will burn like a furnace
under her small-hipped English seat.

Blind with pain she limps home.
The thoroughbred has stood on her foot.
He rested there like a building.
He grew into her foot until they were one.
The marks of the horseshoe printed
into her flesh, the tips of her toes
ripped off like pieces of leather,
three toenails swirled like shells
and left to float in blood in her riding boot.

Blind with fear, she sits on the toilet,
her foot balanced over the washbasin,
her father, hydrogen peroxide in hand,
performing the rites of the cleansing.
She bites on a towel, sucked in breath,
sucked in and arched against the pain,
her eyes glancing off me where
I stand at the door, eyes locked
on the ceiling, eyes of a stranger,
and then she cries . . .
*Oh my God, help me!*
Where a child would have cried *Mama!*
Where a child would have believed *Mama!*
she bit the towel and called on God
and I saw her life stretch out . . .
I saw her torn in childbirth,
and I saw her, at that moment,
in her own death and I knew that she
knew.

*Anne Sexton*

# Poem to My Daughter

'I think I'm going to have it,'
I said, joking between pains.
The midwife rolled competent
sleeves over corpulent milky arms.
'Dear, you never have it,
we deliver it.'
A judgement years proved true.
Certainly I've never had you

as you still have me, Caroline.
Why does a mother need a daughter?
Heart's needle – hostage to fortune –
freedom's end. Yet nothing's more perfect
than that bleating, razor-shaped cry
that delivers a mother to her baby.
The bloodcord snaps that held
their sphere together. The child,
tiny and alone, creates the mother.

A woman's life is her own
until it is taken away
by a first particular cry.
Then she is not alone
but a part of the premises
of everything there is.
A branch, a tide . . . a war.
When we belong to the world
we become what we are.

*Anne Stevenson*

## At Seven a Son

In cold weather on a
garden swing, his legs
in wellingtons rising over
the winter rose trees

he sits serenely
smiling like a Thai
his coat open, his gloves
sewn to the flapping sleeves

his thin knees working
with his arms
folded about the
metal struts

as he flies up
(his hair like long
black leaves) he
lies back freely

astonished in
sunshine as serious
as a stranger he is
a bird in his own thought.

*Elaine Feinstein*

# Do a Dance for Daddy

Do a dance for Daddy, make your Daddy smile
Be his little angel
Remember you're on trial
Mummy's competition, Mummy brings you down
When you're up there shining
She always wears a frown

Do a dance for Daddy. Bend and dip and whirl
You've got all that talent
'Cause you're Daddy's girl
Daddy is your hero, witty and superb
With a sign upon his door
That reads 'DO NOT DISTURB'

Look your best for Daddy
Pass your test for Daddy
Stand up tall for Daddy
Do it all for Daddy

Some day when you're older you will find romance
Someone just like Daddy
Will whistle and you'll dance
You'll recall that music when you're on the shelf
You danced for all the Daddies
But you never found yourself

Paint your eyes for Daddy
Win a prize for Daddy
Swim to France for Daddy
Do your dance for Daddy

*Fran Landesman*

# Mother

I have a happy nature,
But Mother is always sad,
I enjoy every moment of my life, –
Mother has been had.

Stevie Smith

# Men

When I was young, I used to
Watch behind the curtains
As men walked up and down
The street. Wino men, old men.
Young men sharp as mustard.
See them. Men are always
Going somewhere.
They knew I was there. Fifteen
Years old and starving for them.
Under my window, they would pause,
Their shoulders high like the
Breasts of a young girl,
Jacket tails slapping over
Those behinds,
Men.
One day they hold you in the
Palms of their hands, gentle, as if you
Were the last raw egg in the world. Then
They tighten up. Just a little. The
First squeeze is nice. A quick hug.
Soft into your defencelessness. A little
More. The hurt begins. Wrench out a
Smile that slides around the fear. When the
Air disappears,
Your mind pops, exploding fiercely, briefly,
Like the head of a kitchen match. Shattered.
It is your juice
That runs down their legs. Staining their shoes.
When the earth rights itself again,
And taste tries to return to the tongue,
Your body has slammed shut. Forever.
No keys exist.

Then the window draws full upon
Your mind. There, just beyond

The sway of the curtains, men walk.
Knowing something.
Going someplace.
But this time, you will simply
Stand and watch.

Maybe.

*Maya Angelou*

# The Woman in the Ordinary

The woman in the ordinary pudgy downcast girl
is crouching with eyes and muscles clenched.
Round and pebble smooth she effaces herself
under ripples of conversation and debate.
The woman in the block of ivory soap
has massive thighs that neigh,
great breasts that blare and strong arms that trumpet.
The woman of the golden fleece
laughs uproariously from the belly
inside the girl who imitates
a Christmas card virgin with glued hands,
who fishes for herself in others' eyes,
who stoops and creeps to make herself smaller.
In her bottled up is a woman peppery as curry,
a yam of a woman of butter and brass,
compounded of acid and sweet like a pineapple,
like a handgrenade set to explode,
like goldenrod ready to bloom.

*Marge Piercy*

# The Assignation

I have fastened everything within a black cloak.
I am very pale, my look ecstatic.
And in my eyes I hold a split star.
Two red triangles in my hieratic face!

Notice I don't even wear one jewel,
nor a pink bow, nor a spray of dahlias.
And I have even removed the rich buckles
from the straps of my two sandals.

But I am this night, without gold or silks,
slender and dark like a vivid iris.
And I am anointed all over with the oils of nard,
and I am smooth all over beneath this gruff cloak.

And in my pale mouth the trembling carnation
of my kiss already in flower awaits your mouth.
And desire twists in my long hands
like a crazy invisible streamer.

Undress me, lover! Undress me!
Under your glance I will rise like a
vibrant statue on a black plinth
toward which the moon drags itself like a dog.

*Juana de Ibarbourou*
*translated by Brian Swann*

i would write a love story. one to warm my shoulders in this cold room. one of strong brown arms, fine fingers, that happily touch me all over my body. of lips that had to learn to kiss, of nights we lie next to one another, curled, of looking at each other when we are desperate to see one another.

i would write of such a love, such a body, such a person that loves me so. i would write, & be glad, & forget that i sit alone in this room, with no one to come see me.

remember instead the ringing telephone, the soft low voice, the promise of naked warmth. i want my breasts against his chest. i want his hands on my hips, moving smoothly down the curve of my hips as i breathe in his smell. i am tired of people finding each other ugly. i want to sing the beauty of all bodies, of the joy of touch, the warmth & softness of heavy bodies, the tight energy of hard bodies, the soft, melting breasts of mothers; the small buds of breasts of girls. the soft curled cocks of men before they want me; the way they fill & rise to fill me up with their love. the curve of the butt below the balls as he lies on his back, smiling at me, his cock moist & hot. his smooth brown chest, belly flat below his risen cock. the beauty of my soft white breasts coming down on him, my full thighs around his tiny hips. the textures, the colours, the hard places & the soft places, the strength of our bodies as we come together

his tongue licking my breast as he rubs me; my finger touching inside his precious circle – the precious circle that guards his cock but pulls back for me, pulls back when he enters me, so that we are both fully exposed, & vulnerable to each others love.

*Alta*

To the Tune of
'Red Embroidered Shoes'

If you don't know how, why pretend?
Maybe you can fool some girls,
But you can't fool Heaven.
I dreamed you'd play with the
Lotus blossom under my green jacket,
Like a eunuch with a courtesan.
But lo and behold
All you can do is mumble.
You've made me all wet and slippery,
But no matter how hard you try
Nothing happens. So stop.
Go and make somebody else
unsatisfied .

*Huang O*
*translated from the Chinese by*
*Ling Chung and Kenneth Rexroth*

# I Told You When We Started This Relationship What to Expect

. . . I've got this very bad problem.
You see
I can't feel anything
oh except
maybe down there from time to time.

I had a pretty ropy adolescence –
I had you know this really oppressive demanding mother
I had acne; I wanked all the time;
I was scared of girls, no confidence . . .
(no you really don't have to reassure me
I haven't worried about that sort of thing
for years)
anyway
I had a kind of nervous breakdown
when I was eighteen . . .

– and since then?
well, ups and down you know, like everyone else –

except, once or twice (no don't ask me about it I
don't want to be more specific)
I actually got hurt
(no don't put your arm round me, I'm fine now
nobody can hurt me now
you can't, for one)

But I do want some understanding
sometimes I get a bit
well, down –
but you're not to take advantage, play any silly
games . . .

on those days, I might like to go to bed a bit earlier
and stay a bit later the next morning
but you won't actually remind me about it
afterwards
if you're wise . . .

Anyway, I got sidetracked –
the main point is
don't expect to much in the way of feelings. That's
how I am
We can sleep together from time to time
Whenever I want to

and talking –
yes of course we'll talk
interesting talks about things like
your poetry and my work
and yes gossip about friends

and we'll do interesting things too –
When I'm free, and not too tired.
we can eat out sometimes
          where they have
Candles, chrysanths and soy sauce bottles
on the tables –
and go to late night films and meet
our other friends shivering in the queue
                even turn up at
the odd meeting together
          walks perhaps
                  parties . . .
if your behaviour's not too primitive . . .

. . . sex with other people? Well, of course!
Look, you're quite free –
I do not go in for
petty-bourgeois couple restrictions . . . I mean
isn't that what I've just been saying?

Sometimes you surprise me you know
for a feminist you have some really weird ideas . . .

And that reminds me:
Independence. I'll tell you straight.
I'm not into women
who don't lead their own lives
strongly, from their own centre.
I want someone who's got no fears about being alone –
(What do you mean, I'm here now and have been
the last few nights? Well? Well . . . you can explain that one
        later.)
I want you to be independent
and available (within reason of course
you'll have to do other things from time to time).

. . . What the fuck do you mean, contradictory?
I'm perfectly reasonable! You must never
never let anybody dictate your life to you –
I mean
I respect your inner life,
I respect that you're different from me . . .
I read your poems, don't I?

All I want is for you to do the same . . .
Mutual respect.
Well, I can't do it for you,
no, that's something you've got to do by yourself.
I can only be your friend.

– What do you mean, a millstone?
Me? I run a fucking creche two days a week –
I practically founded the Men's Group round here,
I've been into women's problems for years.
– No, I don't find that funny, are you drunk?
Well stop laughing then. What was that?
I make up the rules?
You're fucking jealous, that's your trouble,

and hysterical and insecure,
colonising, possessive –

No, no that would be stupid. No, look . . .
You're not being at all reasonable . . .
Listen, why don't I put the kettle on? Eh?

. . . Oh and, er
look there's just one thing I did want to ask
– er, about . . . um . . . coming, are you . . .
Well is it . . . um . . . just difficult with me
Or do you actually . . . have orgasms
with other people? I mean, more easily . . .

Well, it's not pleasant
to have to ask.

Oh.

Well, I'll just make the tea.

*Stephanie Smolensky*

# Seduction

one day
you gonna walk in this house
and i'm gonna have on a long African
gown
you'll sit down and say 'The Black . . .'
and i'm gonna take one arm out
then you – not noticing me at all – will say 'What about
this brother . . .'
and i'm going to be slipping it over my head
and you'll rapp on about 'The revolution . . .'
while i rest your hand against my stomach
you'll go on – as you always do – saying
'I just can't dig . . .'
while i'm moving your hand up and down
and i'll be taking your dashiki off
then you'll say 'What we really need . . .'
and i'll be licking your arm
and 'The way I see it we ought to . . .'
and unbuckling your pants
'And what about the situation . . .'
and taking your shorts off
then you'll notice
your state of undress
and knowing you you'll just say
'Nikki,
isn't this counterrevolutionary . . .?'

*Nikki Giovanni*

# Rape Poem

There is no difference between being raped
and being pushed down a flight of cement steps
except that the wounds also bleed inside.

There is no difference between being raped
and being run over by a truck
except that afterward men ask if you enjoyed it.

There is no difference between being raped
and being bit on the ankle by a rattlesnake
except that people ask if your skirt was short
and why you were out alone anyhow.

There is no difference between being raped
and going head first through a windshield
except that afterward you are afraid`
not of cars
but half the human race.

The rapist is your boyfriend's brother.
He sits beside you in the movies eating popcorn.
Rape fattens on the fantasies of the normal male
like a maggot in garbage.

Fear of rape is a cold wind blowing
all of the time on a woman's hunched back.
Never to stroll alone on a sand road through pine woods,
never to climb a trail across a bald
without that aluminum in the mouth
when I see a man climbing toward me.

Never to open the door to a knock
without that razor just grazing the throat.
The fear of the dark sides of hedges,
the back seat of the car, the empty house
rattling keys like a snake's warning.

The fear of the smiling man
in whose pocket is a knife.
The fear of the serious man
in whose fist is locked hatred.

All it takes to cast a rapist to be able to see your body
as jackhammer, as blowtorch, as adding-machine-gun.
All it takes is hating that body
your own, your self, your muscle that softens to flab.

All it takes is to push what you hate,
what you fear on to the soft alien flesh.
To bucket out invincible as a tank
armoured with treads without senses
to possess and punish in one act,
to rip up pleasure, to murder those who dare
live in the leafy flesh open to love.

*Marge Piercy*

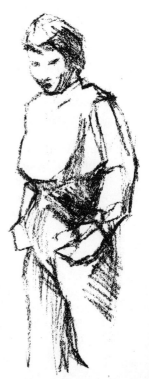

penus envy, they call it
think how handy to have a thing
that poked out; you could just shove
it in any body,    whang whang & come,
wouldn't have to give a shit.
you *know* you'd come!
wouldn't have to love that person,
trust that person.
whang, whang & come.
if you couldn't get relief for free,
pay a little $,    whang whang & come.
you wouldn't have to keep, or abort.
wouldn't have to care about the kid.
wouldn't fear sexual violation.
penus envy, they call it.
the man is sick in his heart.
that's what I call it.

*Alta*

# 'Vagina' Sonnet

Is 'vagina' suitable for use
in a sonnet? I don't suppose so.
A famous poet told me, 'Vagina's ugly.'
Meaning, of course, the *sound* of it. In poems.
Meanwhile he inserts his penis frequently
into his verse, calling it, seriously, 'My
Penis'. It *is* short, I know, and dignified.
I mean of course the sound of it. In poems.
This whole thing is unfortunate, but petty,
like my hangup concerning English Dept. memos
headed 'Mr/Mrs/Miss' – only a fishbone
In the throat of the revolution –
a waste of brains – to be concerned about
this minor issue of my cunt's good name.

*Joan Larkin*

# The Applicant

First, are you our sort of a person?
Do you wear
A glass eye, false teeth or a crutch,
A brace or a hook,
Rubber breasts or a rubber crotch,

Stitches to show something's missing? No, no? Then
How can we give you a thing?
Stop crying
Open your hand.
Empty? Empty. Here is a hand

To fill it and willing
To bring teacups and roll away headaches
And do whatever you tell it.
Will you marry it?
It is guaranteed

To thumb shut your eyes at the end
And dissolve of sorrow
We make new stock from the salt
I notice you are stark naked.
How about this suit –

Black and stiff, but not a bad fit.
Will you marry it?
It is waterproof, shatterproof, proof
against fire and bombs through the roof.
Believe me, they'll bury you in it.

Now your head, excuse me, is empty.
I have the ticket for that.
Come here, sweetie, out of the closet.
Well, what do you think of *that*?
Naked as paper to start

But in twenty-five years she'll be silver,
In fifty, gold.
A living doll, wherever you look.
It can sew, it can cook,
It can talk, talk, talk.

It works, there is nothing wrong with it
You have a hole, it's a poultice.
You have an eye, it's an image
My boy, it's your last resort.
Will you marry it, marry it, marry it.

*Sylvia Plath*

# Penelope

In the pathway of the sun,
   In the footsteps of the breeze,
Where the world and sky are one,
   He shall ride the silver seas,
      He shall cut the glittering wave.
I shall sit at home, and rock;
Rise, to heed a neighbour's knock;
Brew my tea, and snip my thread;
Bleach the linen for my bed.
   They will call him brave.

*Dorothy Parker*

# Nervous Prostration

I married a man of the Croydon class
When I was twenty-two
And I vex him, and he bores me
Till we don't know what to do!
It isn't good form in the Croydon class
To say you love your wife,
So I spend my days with the tradesmen's books
and pray for the end of life.

In green fields are blossoming trees
And a golden wealth of gorse,
And the young birds sing for joy of worms:
It's perfectly clear of course,
That it wouldn't be taste in the Croydon class
To sing over dinner or tea:
But I sometimes wish the gentleman
would turn and talk to me!

But every man of the Croydon class
Lives in terror of joy and speech.
'Words are betrayers', 'Joys are brief' –
The maxims their wise ones teach –
And for all my labour of love and life
I shall be clothed and fed,
And they'll give me an orderly funeral
When I'm still enough to be dead.

*Anna Wickham*

# The Marital Problem

Be White Man's Slave.

White Man be nice sometimes, oh yeah.
Vacuum clean floors and play cards
With children on holiday.

White Man be in fucking bad mood
And swear bad words
Many days.

White Man not accept sloppy work.
White Man not accept fried meat.
White Man not accept stupid talk.
White Man have big fit.
Stumble children's boots

Be White Man's slave

Bear Another Man's children.
Bear White Man's children.
White Man take care
Pay for all the children
Never be free Great Debt
To White Man,

White Man make money at his works
White Man buy things
White Man buy wife.

Wife wash sauce
Wife cook dirt
Wife do dregs
Be White Man's slave.

White Man think many thoughts, become crazy?
Be White Man's slave.
White Man get drunk break things?
Be White Man's slave.

White Man become tired old breast old stomach
White Man tired old lady
Ask go to Hell?
White Man become tired Other Man's children?

Be White Man's slave
Come crawling knees
Begging
Be White Man's slave.

*Sonja Akesson*
*translated from the Swedish by Joanna Bankier*

# The Ache of Marriage

The ache of marriage:

thigh and tongue, beloved,
are heavy with it,
it throbs in the teeth

We look for communion
and are turned away, beloved,
each and each

It is leviathan and we
in its belly
looking for joy, some joy
not to be known outside it

two by two in the ark of
the ache of it.

*Denise Levertov*

# The Long Tunnel of Wanting You

This is the long tunnel of wanting you.
Its walls are lined with remembered kisses
wet & red as the inside of your mouth,
full & juicy as your probing tongue,
warm as your belly against mine,
deep as your navel leading home,
soft as your sleeping cock beginning to stir,
tight as your legs wrapped around mine,
straight as your toes pointing toward the bed
as you roll over & thrust your hardness
into the long tunnel of my wanting,
seeding it with dreams & unbearable hope,
making memories of the future,
straightening out my crooked past,
teaching me to live in the present present tense
with the past perfect and the uncertain future
suddenly certain for certain
in the long tunnel of my old wanting
which before always had an ending
but now begins & begins again
with you, with you, with you.

*Erica Jong*

# In Confidence
*(for the Writers' Group)*

– An orgasm is like an anchovy,
she says,
little, long, and very salty.

– No, it's a caterpillar,
undulating, fat and sweet.

– A sunburst, says the third,
an exploding watermelon:
I had one at Christmas.

– Your body betrays, she says,
one way or another.
Rash and wriggling, it comes
and comes, while your mind
says lie low, or go.

–Or else it snarls and shrinks
to the corner of its cage
while your mind, consenting,
whips it on and out,
out in the open
and *so* free.

– As for me,
says the last,
if I have them brazen
with birthday candles,
with water faucets
or the handles of Toby Jugs,
I don't care who knows it.
But how few I have –
keep *that* in the dark.

*Alison Fell*

## Period Madness

Oh, when the taps jut
and piano stools leap to bite
and your thighs – fat waterbags –
bruise to rainbows, and,
balance gone,
you twirl in a cauldron
reeking of nastiness,
and the spine shrieks
and neglect aches
and time is a swamp to crawl through
till the tide bursts,
and you steam up the street
with elbows angled,
taking swathes –
See me, I am a plougher
of men on the packed pavements,
greasy, snarling,
ready to flail.

*Alison Fell*

This year
I am wearing the more fully-fashioned
bosom.

My husband says
it's due to his attentions.

I say
I'm over thirty.
Time to spread out.
Get comfortable.

*Barbara A Zanditon*

# Aging

*(balm for a 27th birthday)*


Hooked for two years now on wrinkle creams      creams for
crowsfeet      ugly lines (if only there were one!)
any perfumed grease      which promises      youth      beauty
not truth      but all I need on earth
        I've been studying      how women age

                      how

it starts around the eyes      so you can tell
a woman of  22 from one of  28 merely by
a faint scribbling near the lids      a subtle crinkle
        a fine line
extending from the fields of vision

                   this

in itself is not unbeautiful      promising
        as it often does
insights which clear-eyed 22 has no inkling of
promising      certain sure-thighed things in bed
certain fingers on your spine & lids

                 but

it's only the beginning      as ruin proceeds downward
lingering for a while around the mouth      hardening the
        smile
into prearranged patterns (irreversible!)      writing furrows
from the wings of the nose      (oh nothing much at first
        but 'showing promise'      like your early poems

               of deepening)

& plotting lower to the corners of the mouth      drooping
          them
a little      like the tragic mask      though not at all grotesque
as yet      & then as you sidestep      into the 4th decade
beginning to crease the neck      (just slightly)
                though the breasts below

                                                especially

when they're small (like mine) may stay high far
                into the thirties
still the neck will give you away      & after that the chin
which      though you may snip it back & hike it up under
your earlobes will never quite love your bones as it once did

                                                though

the belly may be kept firm through numerous pregnancies
by means of sit-ups      jogging      dancing      (think of
          Russian ballerinas)
                & the cunt
as far I know is ageless      possibly immortal      becoming
          simply
more open      more quick to understand      more dry-eyed
          than at 22

                                                which

after all      is what you were dying for      (as you ravaged
islands of turtles      beehives      oysterbeds      the udders of
          cows)
desperate to censor changes which you simply might have
          let play
over you      lying back      listening      opening yourself
                letting the years make love the only way      (poor
          blunderers)

                                                they know

                                                *Erica Jong*

73

## Bloody Pause

this menopause of mine
pauses too frequently
to render me much service:
i want my bloodletting to be gone
after three decades of woman's potency

my cycles are sufficient now
just as they are:
my womb is seasoned
my tubes tied
my ovum spent
my cervix settling down for better things

yet still i bleed from time to time –
only smears and stains
but still escorted by pains and aches
before the blood begins and even afterwards:
my pace slackens
my stomach swells
my shoulders stiffen
my eyelids shut

mistakenly i had assumed
my clockwork periods
had come full circle –
that i could pacify the goddess otherwise –
with poetry perhaps –
so i shall offer up this bloody piece to her

and pause a while

*Astra*

## The Diet

Sat in the pub
Drink flowing free
Everyone's merry
Cept poor old me
I'm starving

I have to sit
in the corner
All quiet
The trouble you see
I'm on a diet
I'm starving

No whisky, no gin
Why did I come in
no ploughman's lunch
like that greedy bunch
I'm starving

Shall I walk to the bar
I won't go too far
Just a pkt of crisps
and one drink
I'm starving

Then I think I'll have
when I've finished this fag
some chicken and chips
in a basket
I'm starving

No I can't keep quiet
I'll shout, Bugger the diet
I'm absolutely starving

*Maureen Burge*

# A Nude by Edward Hopper

*For Margaret Gaul*

The light
drains me of what I might be,
a man's dream
of heat and softness;
or a painter's
– breasts cosy pigeons,
arms gently curved
by a temperate noon.

I am
blue veins, a scar,
a patch of lavender cells,
used thighs and shoulders;
my calves
are as scant as my cheeks,
my hips won't plump
small, shimmering pillows:

but this body
is home, my childhood
is buried here, my sleep
rises and sets inside,
desire
crested and wore itself thin
between these bones –
I live here.

*Lisel Mueller*

# Back to Africa

'Among the Gallas, when a woman grows tired of the cares of housekeeping, she begins to talk incoherently and demean herself extravagantly. This is a sign of the descent of the holy spirit Callo upon her. Immediately, her husband prostrates himself and adores her; she ceases to bear the humble title of wife and is called 'Lord'; domestic duties have no further claim on her, and her will is a divine law.'

– Sir James George Frazer, *The Golden Bough*

Seeing me weary
        of patching the thatch
        of pounding the bread
        of pacing the floor nightly
        with the baby in my arms,

my tall black husband
        (with eyes like coconuts)
        has fallen down on the floor to adore me!
        I curse myself for being born a woman.
        He thinks I'm God!

I mutter incoherently of Friedan, Millet, Greer . . .
        He thinks the spirit
        has descended.
        He calls me 'Lord.'

      ★

Lord, lord, he's weary in his castle now.
        It's no fun living with a God.
        He rocks the baby, patches the thatch
        & pounds the bread.
        I stay out all night with the Spirit.

Towards morning when the Spirit brings me home,
    he's almost too pooped to adore me.
    I lecture him on the nature
    & duties of men.
    'Biology is destiny,' I say.

Already I hear stirrings of dissent.
    He says he could have been a movie star.
    He says he needs a full-time maid.
    He says he never *meant*
    to marry God.

*Erica Jong*

# Three Poems for Women

## 1

This is a poem for a woman doing dishes.
This is a poem for a woman doing dishes.
It must be repeated.
It must be repeated,
again and again,
again and again,
because the woman doing dishes
because the woman doing dishes
has trouble hearing
has trouble hearing.

## 2

And this is another poem for a woman
cleaning the floor
who cannot hear at all.
Let us have a moment of silence
for the woman who cleans the floor.

## 3

And here is one more poem
for the woman at home
with children.
You never see her at night.
Stare at an empty space and imagine her there,
the woman with children
because she cannot be here to speak
for herself,
and listen
to what you think
she might say.

*Susan Griffin*

## An Answer to a Man's Question,
## 'What can I do about Women's Liberation?'

Wear a dress.
Wear a dress that you made yourself, or bought in a dress
      store.
Wear a dress and underneath the dress wear elastic, around
your hips, and underneath your nipples.
Wear a dress and underneath the dress wear a sanitary
      napkin.
Wear a dress and wear sling back, high heeled shoes.
Wear a dress, with elastic and a sanitary napkin underneath,
and sling back shoes on your feet, and walk down Telegraph
Avenue.
Wear a dress, with elastic and a sanitary napkin and sling
back shoes on Telegraph Avenue and try to run.

Find a man.
Find a nice man who you would like to ask you for a date.
Find a nice man who *will* ask you for a date.
Keep your dress on.
Ask the nice man who asks you for a date to come to dinner.
Cook the nice man a nice dinner so the dinner is ready before
he comes and your dress is nice and clean and wear a smile.
Tell the nice man you're a virgin, or you don't have
birth control, or you would like to get to know him better.
Keep your dress on.
Go to the movies by yourself.

Find a job.
Iron your dress.
Wear your ironed dress and promise the boss you won't get
pregnant (which in your case is predictable) and you like to
type, and be sincere and wear your smile.
Find a job or get on welfare.
Borrow a child and get on welfare.

Borrow a child and stay in the house all day with the child,
or go to the public park with the child, and take the child
to the welfare office and cry and say your man left you and
be humble and wear your dress and your smile, and don't talk
back, keep your dress on, cook more nice dinners, stay
away from Telegraph Avenue, and still, you won't know the
half of it, not in a million years.

*Susan Griffin*

# In the Men's Room(s)

When I was young I believed in intellectual conversation:
I thought the patterns we wove on stale smoke
floated off to the heaven of ideas.
To be certified worthy of high masculine discourse
like a potato on a grater I would rub on contempt,
suck snubs, wade proudly through the brown stuff on the
      floor.
They were talking of integrity and existential ennui
while the women ran out for six-packs and had abortions
in the kitchen and fed the children and were auctioned off.

Eventually of course I learned how their eyes perceived me:
when I bore to them cupped in my hands a new poem to
      nibble,
when I brought my aerial maps of Sartre or Marx,
they said, she is trying to attract our attention,
she is offering up her breasts and thighs.
I walked on eggs, their tremulous equal:
they saw a fish peddler hawking in the street.

Now I get coarse when the abstract nouns start flashing.
I go out to the kitchen to talk cabbages and habits.
I try hard to remember to watch what people do.
Yes, keep your eyes on the hands, let the voice go buzzing.
Economy is the bone, politics is the flesh,
watch who they beat and who they eat,
watch who they relieve themselves on, watch who they
      own.
The rest is decoration.

*Marge Piercy*

## *Excerpt from* Monster

I want a women's revolution like a lover.
I lust for it, I want so much this freedom,
this end to struggle and fear and lies
we all exhale, that I could die just
with the passionate uttering of that desire.
Just once in this my only lifetime to dance
all alone and bare on a high cliff under cypress trees
with no fear of where I place my feet.
To even glimpse what I might have been and never never
will become, had I not had to 'waste my life' fighting
for what my lack of freedom keeps me from glimpsing.
Those who abhor violence refuse to admit they are already
experiencing it, committing it.
Those who lie in the arms of the 'individual solution',
the 'private Odyssey', the 'personal growth',
are the most conformist of all,
because to admit suffering is to begin
the creation of freedom.
Those who fear dying refuse to admit they are already dead.
Well, I am dying, suffocating from this hopelessness
          tonight,
from this dead weight of struggling with
even those few men I love and care less about
each day they kill me:

Do you understand? Dying.
          Going crazy.

*Robin Morgan*

# A Woman Defending Herself
## Examines Her Own Character Witness

QUESTION: Who am I?

ANSWER: You are a woman.

Q. How did you come to meet me?

A. I came to meet you through my own pain and suffering.

Q. How long have you known me?

A. I feel I have known you since my first conscious
moment.

Q. But how long really?

A. Since my first conscious moment – for four years.

Q. How old are you?

A. Thirty-one years old.

Q. Will you explain this to the court?

A. I was not conscious until I met you through my own
pain and suffering.

Q. And this was four years ago?

A. This was four years ago.

Q. Why did it take you so long?

A. I was told lies

Q. What kind of lies?

A. Lies about you.

Q. Who told you these lies?

A. Everyone. Most only repeating the lies they were told.

Q. And how did you find out the truth?

A. I did not. I only stopped hearing lies.

Q. No more lies were told?

A. Oh no. The lies are still told, but I stopped hearing
them.

Q. Why?

A. My own feelings became too loud.

Q. You could not silence your own feelings any longer?

A. That is correct.

Q. What kind of woman am I?

Q. You are a woman I recognise.

Q. How do you recognise me?

A.  You are a woman who is angry.
    You are a woman who is tired.
    You are a woman who receives letters from her
        children.
    You are a woman who was raped.
    You are a woman who speaks too loudly.
    You are a woman without a degree.
    You are a woman with short hair.
    You are a woman who takes her mother home from the
        hospital.
    You are a woman who reads books about other
        women.
    You are a woman whose light is on at four in the
        morning.
    You are a woman who wants more.
    You are a woman who stopped in her tracks.
    You are a woman who will not say please.
    You are a woman who has had enough.
    You are a woman clear in your rage.
    And they are afraid of you
    I know
    they are afraid of you.
Q.  This last must be stricken from the record as the witness
        does not know it for a fact.
A.  I know it for a fact that they are afraid of you.
Q.  How do you know?
A.  Because of the way they tell lies about you.
Q.  If you go on with this line you will be instructed to
        remain silent.
A.  And that is what they require of us.

                                        *Susan Griffin*

# For My 'Apolitical' Sisters

i am so *hostile* you say
when i struggle to break my chains

i am so *extreme* you say
when i say all women are oppressed

i am *unrealistic* and *impractical*, even *mad* you say
when i say we must consciously refuse to take care of men

i have become so *political* you say . . .
sister, i've got news for you:
your 'inactivity' is also a political statement . . .

listen:
oppression is not a choice
or just the misfortune of the socially deprived
no woman has escaped
sexism falls like quiet rain
constantly, softly seeping in
until we all become saturated
and it gently, ever so gently
so we hardly notice
does us terrible violence,
the ice forms, moulding us into
a shape uncannily uniform, uncannily
suitable for men.
oppression is not a choice, to fight it IS
we must stir the springs of liquid fire
in every woman, every child,
flames to burn the last wail of male arrogance
from our minds and hearts and bodies.

until then
when you nurture his ego, offer your body,
wash his socks, raise his children,
you are being a political activist too.

*Aspen*

# Objets d'Art

When I was seventeen, a man in the Dakar Station
Men's Room (I couldn't read the signs) said to me:
You're a real ball cutter. I thought about that
For months and finally decided
He was right. Once I knew that was my thing,
Or whatever we would have said in those days,
I began to perfect my methods. Until then
I had never thought of trophies. Preservation
Was at first a problem: pickling worked
But was a lot of trouble. Freezing
Proved to be the answer. I had to buy
A second freezer just last year; the first
Was filled with rows and rows of
Pink and purple lumps encased in Saran wrap.

I have more subjects than I can handle,
But only volunteers. It is an art like hypnosis
Which cannot be imposed on the unwilling victim.
If you desire further information about the process and
The benefits, please drop in any night from nine to twelve.
My place is east of Third on Fifty-sixth.
You'll know it by the three gold ones over the door.

*Cynthia MacDonald*

*From* Notes from the First Year
*for my sisters, a trilogy of revolution*


Questionnaire


There is unfeminine (but oh, so Female)
sureness in my hands,
checking 'No.' to every question
in the Harris poll. Reader's Digest,
        Mademoiselle.
I am an outlaw, so none of that applies to me:
I do not vote in primaries, do not wish to increase
        my spending power, do not take birth control
        pills.
I do not have a legal residence, cannot tell you
        my given name or how (sometimes very) old
        I really am.
I do not travel abroad, see no humour in uniforms,
        and my lips are good enough for my lover
        as they are.
Beyond that, no one heads my household, I would not
        save my marriage if I had one, or anybody else's
        if I could.
I do not believe that politicians need me, that Jesus
        loves me, or that short men are particularly sexy.
Nor do I want a penis.
What else do you have to offer?

*Susan Saxe*

# To Phil (if he wakes up)

Anger
Anger drove me to it
I killed him at last
One night when we were alone in the house
And the stage was set for sex
And romance
and he fell asleep,
smelling of creosote and beer.
So I killed him. It was simple really
with a knife I had from the Guides
It was sharp and strong
So I found his heart and looked at him, sleeping and
      unaware
he'd always said he wanted to die in his sleep
the irony was good
I smiled at him once and the knife slid in, meeting resistance
      of flesh at first
and then something that felt like gristle under my butcher's
      knife in the kitchen
He looked up once before he died
And his eyes had that wide open, slightly surprised look of
      just before he came
and his tongue hung out like it always did
and then his body twitched and he died.

*Kath McKay*

## The Petals of the Tulips

The petals of the tulips
just before they open

when they're pulling
the last dark purple energy through the stem

are covered with a whitish veil,
a caul.

I like them best then:

they're me the month before I was born

the month Mother spent
flat on here back in the hospital.

The way I found out –

once, in round eight of one of our fights
I hissed at her, 'I didn't ask to be born!'

and she threw back her head and howled,
remembering,

'You? You?

Hot as it was that summer
I had to lie there for weeks
hanging on to you.

You? You were begging to be born!'

*Judith Hemschemeyer*

# First Love

You were tall and beautiful.
You wore your long brown hair
wound about your head,
your neck stood clear and full
as the stem of a vase.
You held my hand in yours
and we walked slowly, talking
of small familiar happenings
and of the lost secrets of
your childhood. It seems it was

Always autumn then.
The amber trees shook. We laughed
in a wind that cracked the leaves
from black boughs and set them scuffling
about our feet, for me to trample still
and kick in orange clouds
about your face. We would climb dizzy
to the cliff's edge and stare down
at a green and purple sea, the

Wind howling in our ears, as it
tore the breath from white cheeked waves.
You steadied me against
the wheeling screech of gulls, and i
loved to think that but for your strength
i would tumble to the rocks below
to the fated death, your stories made me
dream of. i don't remember
that i looked in your eyes or that we
ever asked an open question. Our thoughts

Passed through our blood, it seemed,
and the slightest pressure of our hands
decided all issues wordlessly.
We watched in silence by the shore
the cold spray against our skin,

in mutual need of the water's fierce,
inhuman company, that gave promise
of some future, timeless refuge from
all the fixed anxieties of our world.
As we made for home

We faced into the wind, my thighs
were grazed by its icy teeth, you
gathered your coat about me and i
hurried our steps towards home, fire
and the comfort of your sweet strong tea.
We moved bound in step.
You sang me songs of Ireland's sorrows
and of proud women, loved and lost.
I knew then, they set for me
a brilliant stage of characters, who

Even now, can seem more real
than my most intimate friends.
We walked together, hand in hand.
You were tall and beautiful,
you wore your long brown hair wound
about your head, your neck stood
clear and full as the stem of a vase.
I was young – you were my mother
and it seems, it was always
autumn then.

*Mary Dorcey*

## Back You Come

Back you come mother dear
to walk with me in my woods
and see my brook
and cut my pussy willows
and drink pots of tea in my warm kitchen
let me hold your hand
and brush your petaled hair
as Adam brushes mine these days
when he's not leaning my head against
his small shoulder
as I cry
back you come mother dear
to fill up some of the longing
I always felt you felt:
yearning yearning for less
complicated complications such as
parenthood livelihood wifehood
yearnings for countryside quietness
and honeysuckled nighttimes
and firebright laughter
with no contradictions from me
and no competition for you
in the form of relations or friends
of mine:
no reality intruding

back you come mother dear
to your vision of you and me
as sisters
but this time let's make it realler
with no power games:
you really running the show
and me acquiescing
just to keep the peace
this time let's have it

a little more equal
allowing you to be you
and me to be me
and both to be different if need be

still want to come back
mother dear?

*Astra*

# For My Mother's Mother

Driving with my mother
from Chicago to Boston,
only ourselves to talk to.
In a snow storm between Buffalo and Syracuse
she told me quietly
how her mother died.


I was eight and Lorraine was four.
Lorraine was a difficult child.
We moved a lot because of Daddy's job
but he had finally promised Mother they would settle.
They built a home in the country
with window seats and flagstone fireplace.
We moved in.
Three weeks later Daddy's company wanted him to move
        again.
He went.
Mother was going to pack and follow.
But Lorraine was a difficult child
and Mother was pregnant again.
She couldn't face moving and having another child
so she went to her mother and aunt.
Grandma Andersen told her something,
gave her something,
I don't know,
from the old country.
It didn't work.
She was sick.
I heard her screams from the next room
but they wouldn't let me go in.
By the time Daddy got home she was dead.


He never knew what happened or how she died.
What do you mean, I asked?
How could he not know?

Didn't he care? Didn't he ask?
They just told him it was a woman's problem.
He never knew. After he died
Grandma Andersen told Lorraine and she told me.
All I remembered was the house
where my mother died
and how she cried
and they finally took Lorraine and me away
so we wouldn't hear.

For two years now
I have heard my mother's mother's screams.
They are all I know of her
they are with me.
I have listened to her screams
as they became my own.
I have lived through her death.
Untold, yet I know how she did it.
She took some poison
when that didn't work
she shoved something up her vagina.
And that worked and she bled
and expelled and was infected
and poisoned and she died.
I have heard her screams of pain
splutter through her clenched teeth
and grow weaker.
I have heard her screams of rage
deep in my chest
as she cursed her husband
and her mother
and Lorraine who was always a difficult child
and herself who could not cope,
who should have been different
or better
or more able to manage these things somehow.

I asked, a year later: what was her name?
Whose?
Your mother, my grandmother,
what was her name?
Judith, she said.
I named my first daughter after my mother.

*Judith McDaniel*

# Miss Rosie

When I watch you
wrapped up like garbage
sitting, surrounded by the smell
of too old potato peels
or
when I watch you
in your old man's shoes
with the little toe cut out
sitting, waiting for your mind
like next week's grocery
I say
when I watch you
you wet brown bag of a woman
who used to be the best looking gal in Georgia
used to be called the Georgia Rose
I stand up
through your destruction
I stand up

*Lucille Clifton*

## The Woman Who Swims in Her Tears

The woman who swims in her tears
the woman who dives down deep
                            in her weeping, the
woman who floats downstream in
                            her grieving, the
woman who lives in the depths of her
                                        crying
                                    of her aching
                                    of her holding
                                        herself
                    with her own arms
                    and rocking, the
woman who has no mother, the
woman who mothers,
the woman filled with love
who looks at herself
through a closed glass window
and wonders why she cannot touch.

The woman
who slept beside the body of one
other woman weeping,
the women who wept.
the women whose tears wet
    each other's hair
the woman who wrapped her legs
    around another woman's thigh
  and said I am afraid.
the woman who put her head
    in the
place between the shoulder and breast
    of the other woman and
    said, 'Am I wrong?'
the women who wept together
the women who pressed

their faces together
their hands together
their eyes together
their thighs together
who pressed into each other
who cried together
who cried
who cried out
who cried out joy
the women who
cried out joy
together.

*Susan Griffin*

# Magnificat

*(for Sian, after thirteen years)*

oh this man
what a meal he made of me
how he chewed and gobbled and sucked
in the end he spat me all out

you arrived on the dot, in the nick
of time, with your red curls flying
I was about to slip down the sink like grease
I nearly collapsed, I almost
wiped myself out like a stain
I called for you, and you came, you voyaged
fierce as a small archangel with swords and breasts
you declared the birth of a new life
in my kitchen there was an annunciation
and I was still, awed by your hair's glory

you commanded me to sing of my redemption

oh my friend, how
you were mother for me, and how
I could let myself lean on you
comfortable as an old cloth
familiar as enamel saucepans
I was a child again, pyjama'ed
in winceyette, my hair plaited, and you

listened, you soothed me like cake and milk
you listened to me for three days, and I poured
it out, I flowed all over you like wine, like oil
you touched the place where it hurt
at night, we slept together in my big bed
your shoulder eased me towards dreams

when we met, I tell you
it was a birthday party, a funeral
it was a holy communion
between women, a Visitation
it was two old she-goats butting
and nuzzling each other in the smelly fold

*Michèle Roberts*

# Thanksgiving

The beauty of
          the male face
acknowledging sorrow
of a man who hurts
and lets you see

I had almost forgotten
          my brothers
when you cried
I had almost
          learned to hate
when your face changed

In that room the air
          stopped being frozen
words stopped
     banging together
and I
   began to move

I never thought
          it would be a man
I thought women were alone
that your hands were
          like steel
until I held on to them

until you closed your eyes
and grief like
          red glass
          illumined you
and I could see again
with doubled vision

                    *Sharon Barba*

## The Truce Between the Sexes

For a long time unhappy
with my man,
I blamed men,
blamed marriage, blamed
the whole bleeding world,
because I could not lie in bed with him
without lying to him
or else to myself
& lying to myself
became increasingly hard
as my poems
struck rock.

My life & my poems lived apart;
I had to marry them,
& marrying them
meant divorcing him,
divorcing the lie.

Now I lie in bed
with my poems on the sheets
& a man I love
sleeping or reading
at my side.

Because I love him,
I do not think of him
as 'Men',
but as my friend
Hate generalises;
love is particular.

He is not Men, man, male–
all those maddening m's
muttering like machine-gun spittle,

but only a person like me,
dreaming, vulnerable, scared,
his dreams
opening into rooms
where the chairs
are wishes you can sit on
& the rugs are wonderful
with oriental birds.

The first month we lived together
I was mad with joy,
thinking that a person with a penis
could dream, tell jokes, even cry . . .
Now I find it usual,
& when other women sputter
of their rage,
I look at them blankly,
half comprehending
those poor mediaeval creatures
from a dark, dark age.

I wonder about myself.
Was I always so fickle?
Must politics always be personal?

If I struck oil,
would I crusade
for depletion allowances?

Erica, Erica,
you are hard on yourself.
Lie back & enjoy the cease-fire.
Trouble will come again.
Sex will grow horns & warts.
The white sheets of this bed
will be splattered with blood.
Just wait.

But I don't believe it.
There will be trouble enough,
but a different sort.

*Erica Jong*

# A Decision

I am a very mature person
but nobody knows me.
My friends have a wrong idea of me.
I am not tame.
With the talons of an eagle I have weighed tameness.
O eagle, how sweet is the flight of your wings.
Shall you be silent like everything else?
Do you perhaps want to write poetry? You shall never write
      poetry any more.
Each poem shall be the ripping apart of a poem,
not a poem, but the marks of talons.

*Edith Södergran*
*translated from the Swedish by Jaakko A. Ahokas*

# To Julia de Burgos

The people are saying that I am your enemy,
   That in poetry I give you to the world.

   They lie, Julia de Burgos. They lie, Julia de Burgos.
The voice that rises in my verses is not your voice: it is my
      voice;
For you are the clothing and I am the essence;
Between us lies the deepest abyss.

   You are the bloodless doll of social lies
And I the virile spark of human truth;

   You are the honey of courtly hypocrisy; not I –
I bare my heart in all my poems.

   You, like your world, are selfish; not I –
I gamble everything to be what I am.

   You are only the serious lady. Señora. Doña Julia.
Not I. I am life. I am strength. I am woman.

   You belong to your husband, your master. Not I:
I belong to nobody or to all, for to all, to all
I give myself in my pure feelings and thoughts.

   You curl your hair and paint your face. Not I:
I am curled by the wind, painted by the sun.

You are the lady of the house, resigned, submissive,
Tied to the bigotry of men. Not I:
I am Rocinante, bolting free, wildly
Snuffling the horizons of the justice of God.

*Julia de Burgos*
*translated by Grace Schulman*

why do you write they ask
why do you breathe i ask

*Alta*

# The Frozen Sea

A book should be like
an axe to crack
the frozen sea
inside (Kafka said).
You think this is just
a poem, but it is not.
It is the sound of an axe.
I want you to hear that I am tired.
I want you to hear that I am no longer
reasonable. Hear my
footsteps as I enter the bank
and think for two brief seconds
of holding it up. Hear the pages
turn in the bookstore where for
two brief seconds I consider
throwing the book,
across the room. Hear the
rush of soundlessness on
the telephone wires
while my mind hatches
obscenities. Two seconds
can be so
long, I am sus
pended in two
se
conds,
my toes blue with rage,
the top of my head
hot with weeping,
I shudder as the axe
comes down, what
will you do with me
when you hear the blow
where will you put me then?

*Susan Griffin*

i stepped into the ring
cause i thot poet of the people,
responsibility of the voice to listen
to the mind.
very revolutionary i thot.
they beat me up.
dont know what i expected.

*Alta*

## Woman Enough

Because my grandmother's hours
were apple cakes baking,
& dust motes gathering,
& linens yellowing
& seams and hems
inevitably unravelling–
I almost never keep house–
though really I *like* houses
& wish I had a clean one.

Because my mother's minutes
were sucked into the roar
of the vacuum cleaner,
because she waltzed with the washer-dryer
& tore her hair waiting for repairmen–
I send out my laundry,
& live in a dusty house,
though really I *like* clean houses
as well as anyone.

I am woman enough
to love the kneading of bread
as much as the feel
of typewriter keys
under my fingers–
springy, springy.
& the smell of clean laundry
& simmering soup
are almost as dear to me
as the smell of paper and ink.

I wish there were not a choice;
I wish I could be two women.
I wish the days could be longer.
But they are short.

So I write while
the dust piles up.

I sit at my typewriter
remembering my grandmother
& all my mothers,
& the minutes they lost
loving houses better than themselves—
& the man I love cleans up the kitchen
grumbling only a little
because he knows
that after all these centuries
it is easier for him
than for me.

*Erica Jong*

# *from* Placenta Praevia

. . . what of the lonely 7 year old (7½ mommy!) watching
      tv in the front room? what of her?
what of yesterday when she chased the baby into my room
      and I screamed
OUT OUT GET OUT & she ran
right out but the baby stayed,
unafraid. what is it like to have
a child afraid of you, your own
child, your first child, the one
youre expected to be most nervous with, the one no one
      expects
you to be perfect with (except women in parking lots)
who must forgive you if either of you are to survive . . .

& how right is it to shut her out of the room so i can write
about her?
how human, how loving? how can
i even try to
: name her.

*Alta*

121

# White Bear

In 1867
White Bear
a Kiowa Indian
known for his courage
and eloquence
said to the United
States Congress,

*'I have heard that you intend to*
*settle us on a reservation near the*
*mountains. I don't want to settle.*
*I love to roam over the prairies.*
*There I feel free and happy, but*
*when we settle down we grow*
*pale and die.'*

I read this in a museum
White Bear's medicine bag behind
a glass case and me
on the other side
thinking, it is clear
I do not know how to live
anymore words do not
even come to my mouth,
I want to
forget all I
learned
if it has
led to this, these
Indians knew how to
ride ponies at age five,
chew porcupine needles,
use river clay and plant dyes,
and I tell you,
they had beautiful songs to sing.

I press my hand to the glass
and read
White Bear
committed suicide
in a prison
in Huntsville Texas, 1878. What
reward is there
for patience, I slide my
hand on the cool glass
the keeper lets me through the door.
What shall I do now?
I ask, pedaling my bicycle
up the street.

At home
my daughter waits,
the innocent jailor,
together
we grow pale
doing dishes
and answering the telephone.
She runs
twice as much
as I, yells
much louder,
and when she's unhappy
she cries.

I teach her
to beware of
electricity and
fire.
What else she learns,
I am afraid to
name.

*Susan Griffin*

## Love Should Grow Up
## Like a Wild Iris in the Fields

Love should grow up like a wild iris in the fields,
unexpected, after a terrible storm, opening a purple
mouth to the rain, with not a thought to the future,
ignorant of the grass and the graveyard of leaves
around, forgetting its own beginning. Love should
grow like a wild iris
but does not.
Love more often is to be found in kitchens at the dinner
hour,
tired out and hungry, lingers over tables in houses where
the walls record movements; while the cook is probably
angry,
and the ingredients of the meal are budgeted, while
a child cries feed me now and her mother not quite
hysterical says over and over, wait just a bit, just a bit,
love should grow up in the fields like a wild iris
but never does
really startle anyone, was to be expected, was to be
predicted, is almost absurd, goes on from day to day, not
quite
blindly, gets taken to the cleaners every fall, sings old
songs over and over, and falls on the same piece of rug
that
never gets tacked down, gives up, wants to hide, is not
brave, knows too much, is not like an
iris growing wild but more like
staring into space
in the street
not quite sure
which door it was, annoyed about the sidewalk being
slippery, trying all the doors, thinking
if love wished the world to be well, it would be well.
Love should
grow up like a wild iris, but doesn't, it comes from

124

the midst of everything else, sees like the iris
of an eye, when the light is right,
feels in blindness and when there is nothing else is
tender, blinks, and opens
face up to the skies.

*Susan Griffin*


## *From* Placenta Praevia

& all those years nobody loved me
except her & I screamed at her & spanked
her
& threw her on the bed & slammed the
door when
i was angry & desperate for her
father's love,
& I cant undo all those times i frightened her
& she loved me, she still loves me,
i cant undo needing &
being tortured with loneliness
until I cried out at her,
who loved me even in my needy loneliness. & how
do mothers, unloved, love their children?
the wonder is that we do, we
do not leave the little girl, we
do not destroy
we cry out in terror we love
our little girls
who must have a better life . . .

*Alta*

o i want to do it all i want
to drain my tortured mind i
want to hold yr thin body
i want to love the children all
the time, all the time

*Alta*

## Declaration

We forgive our mothers.
We forgive ourselves.
We are good enough,
even if we don't think we're
good enough.
It's safe for us to be ourselves.
We are not afraid to give
the love
that we feel.

*Kamalu and Fan*